27

# Plants Are Like That

by A. Harris Stone
and Irving Leskowitz

**ILLUSTRATED BY PETER P. PLASENCIA**

PRENTICE-HALL, INC., Englewood Cliffs, N. J.

*For Freddy, Joey and Ruthie,*
*but especially for Annie*

*Plants Are Like That* by A. Harris Stone and Irving Leskowitz
© 1968 by A. Harris Stone and Irving Leskowitz

Library of Congress Catalog Card Number: 68-10651
Printed in the United States of America   J

Prentice-Hall International, Inc., London
Prentice-Hall of Australia, Pty. Ltd., Sydney
Prentice-Hall of Canada, Ltd., Toronto
Prentice-Hall of India Private Ltd., New Delhi
Prentice-Hall of Japan, Inc., Tokyo

# CONTENTS

## INTRODUCTION

What do you know about plants?

Everyone knows that plants are green, that they need water and that some plants produce flowers. But there is more to plants than just this! Inside each plant, hundreds of chemical and physical processes take place. All the activities of a plant, from germination to seed formation, are made possible and are controlled by these processes. The chemical and physical reactions occurring inside plants make up what botanists call *plant metabolism*. The way plants obtain and use food, how plants grow, what they do with water, how they obtain and use energy, and how they use light are all part of plant metabolism. In this book you will find many experiments that deal with the metabolic activities of plants.

If you want to learn something about plant metabolism, you will need to work and think as a botanist does.

7

This means, that as you work, you will want to ask yourself the same questions that a botanist would ask:

WHAT HAPPENS?

HOW DOES IT HAPPEN?

WHAT WILL HAPPEN IF I DO THIS?

WHAT HAPPENS IF I CHANGE THE CONDITIONS

Not only botanists, but all scientists ask these questions as they experiment.

You probably know that an experiment is a test. When a scientist experiments, he tries to discover a new fact or idea. With new facts, he tries to explain what he and others have observed. For example, it was well-known for many, many years that sunflowers always face the sun. Some scientists were curious to find out why. They experimented and discovered some facts that helped them explain why sunflowers (and other plants) turn toward the light.

Sometimes scientists may try to prove something people already know or think they know. Often they find that something everyone believes is so is not so.

Remember, a scientist watches his work carefully and always thinks about what he is doing. He isn't afraid to try something new or to do things in a different way. He is not frightened away from doing something because it may turn out to be wrong.

The experiments in this book are not described in detail, so do them as you think they should be done. The pictures will be helpful in giving you starting ideas. Experiments with plants require planning and patience. For most of the experiments in this book, you will need young plants and this means they must be started in advance. Often you will have to wait several hours, or even a day or two, to see the results of an experiment. Don't be discouraged if occasionally an experiment does not work as you think it should. This happens to every scientist at some time. When it does, he carefully repeats the experiment and makes changes where necessary. That's the way to experiment and discover!

Scientists do not trust their memories; they keep accurate notes and records of their work. Follow their example and record your experiment results in a notebook. Describe what you did and what you observed. Before making up your mind or reaching a *conclusion* about an experiment, be certain of your observations. Don't hesitate to repeat an experiment to make certain your first observations were correct.

At the end of this book there is a list of plants and materials that will be useful in doing these experiments.

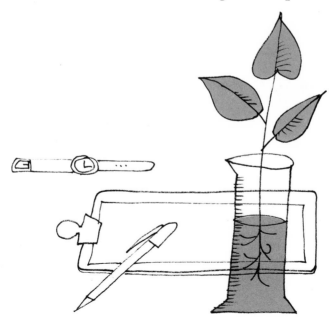

## WATER IN

How does water move into a plant? Does it move from one part of the plant to another? What happens to a piece of celery when it is left out of the refrigerator overnight? What happens to it if it is then placed into a glass of cold water? Will the same thing happen if hot water is used?

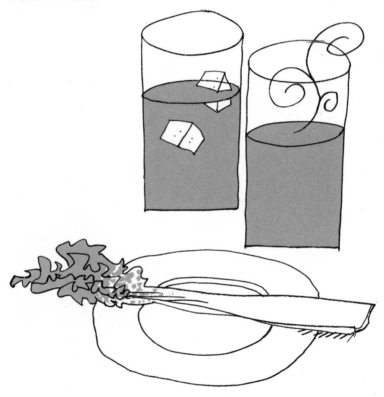

Does the celery stalk that was left out overnight break as easily as one that has been allowed to stand in cold water?

Plants need water for many purposes. It is not only a food for the plant but is needed to help keep the plant standing straight. What can be observed if a stalk of celery that has been left out of the refrigerator overnight is held in an upright position? What can be observed if a stalk of celery that has been standing overnight in a glass of water is held in an upright position? Which one is firmer? The firmness of plants is due to something that botanists call turgidity. The turgidity of plants depends upon the amount of water in the plant. Whan a plant loses water it loses turgidity and becomes softer. What characteristic of a wilted plant would tell you that the wilting is caused by a loss of water? How can a potted plant be made to wilt? How can it be revived?

Can a wilted celery stalk be made turgid by placing it upside down in a glass of water? Would the same thing happen if the leaves were removed before placing the stalk upside down in water?

## MORE WATER IN

How rapidly does water enter a plant? How can colored water be used to help time the speed of the water entering plants? Does the temperature affect the speed with which water enters the plant? After water enters a plant, does it have a special place to go?

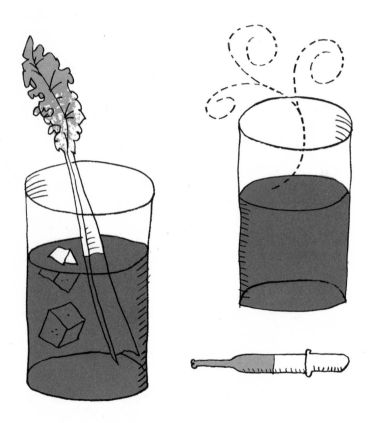

Does this experiment show where the water goes after it has entered the plant?

Water moves through a plant by way of special tube-like structures. When a celery stalk is cut these tubes are opened and water may enter or exit from them. What happens if the cut end of a piece of wilted celery is coated with wax before it is placed into a glass of cold water? Will food coloring in this water be useful in seeing what happens? How is the celery stalk affected by coating the cut end with detergent? Does salad oil have the same effect?

## WATER OUT

Does the water that a plant takes in remain in the plant? What would happen to a plant if all the water that entered it remained inside?

How can the amount of water taken in or given off by a plant be measured by the apparatus shown above?

If some water does escape from the plant, from which part of the plant does it leave?

Water does not pass through a layer of petroleum jelly. How can petroleum jelly help you find out which part of the plant loses water?

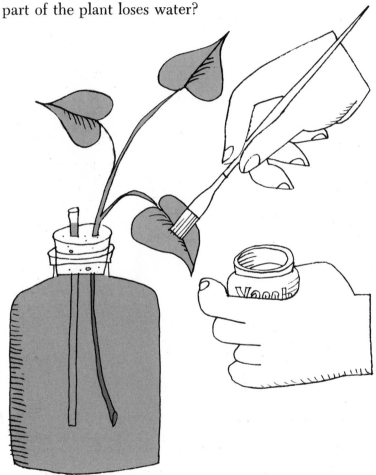

Is more water lost through the top surface of a leaf than through the bottom surface?

## MORE WATER OUT

What controls the speed with which water escapes from a plant? Does the amount of light have any effect? Does the soil of a potted plant dry out more rapidly in the light than it does in the dark?

What can be seen in a plastic bag if the bag is tied around the top of the plant and left for some time? How long does it take for a change to appear?

The loss of water by plants is controlled by many factors. To find out how each factor affects the plant's water loss, it is helpful to set up a number of groups, each containing several plants. Each group is used to test the effect of a single factor. Some factors which can be investigated to see how they affect water loss are humidity, temperature and light. There are probably other factors, too. What experiments can be done to show the effect of each factor on the plant's water loss?

A few words about experimental controls may be helpful here.

If only one plant is used to test each factor, the results may not be reliable. For example, suppose one plant is used to test the effect of a certain chemical and the plant dies. Did it die because of the chemical, or might it have died for some other reason? We could not be sure of the answer if only one plant were used. But if the chemical were used on several plants and all of them died, then we could be *fairly* certain the chemical was responsible. Along with the group of plants being treated with the chemical, there should be another group of plants which are not treated. This group is called the control group. If the plants treated with the chemical died and the experimental controls did not, then we could be *quite* certain that the plants died because of the chemical.

## TAKE A BREATH

Do plants breathe? If they do, do they use the same gases in the air that animals do? What gases do animals use? What happens if you breathe into limewater? What happens to a jar of limewater if it is sealed in a plastic bag with a plant?

What will happen if the bag is not sealed?

The earth's atmosphere is a mixture of gases—nitrogen, oxygen, carbon dioxide and water vapor—plus small amounts of other gases. Of these gases, oxygen and carbon dioxide play the most important roles in breathing. Carbon dioxide can be easily detected by means of a simple chemical test. When carbon dioxide is mixed with limewater, a milky solution is produced.

The air we breathe into our lungs contains a large amount of oxygen and little carbon dioxide. The air we breathe out has much less oxygen and much more carbon dioxide. From this, you can see that in our breathing we are taking oxygen from the air and putting carbon dioxide into the air. Other animals do this, too.

## TAKE ANOTHER BREATH

Does a plant "breathe" at night in the same way it does during the day? How can limewater be used to show that this is happening?

Can you decide which container of limewater is more milky? Can you tell from this that plants "breathe" at different rates at different times of the day?

Geologists and astronomers tell us that when the earth was formed, there was no breathable oxygen in the atmosphere. How did oxygen get into the atmosphere? Many scientists believe that all the oxygen in the atmosphere today was put there by green plants.

Green plants "breathe" the same gases animals do, but in a different way. In the dark, plants use up oxygen and give off carbon dioxide, which is what animals do. But in the light, green plants use up carbon dioxide and give off oxygen. At first there were no green plants on earth, but after they evolved, they began to increase in number. As they did, they produced more and more oxygen. In fact, they are still doing so.

What would happen if all the green plants on earth were to die? Would there be enough food for all the animals? Would carbon dioxide accumulate? Would oxygen be used up?

## THE LAST GASP

How rapidly does a plant give off carbon dioxide? Does the rate differ with the amount of light? What happens to the oil bubble in the straw?

Does temperature affect the rate of carbon dioxide production?

The more oxygen a plant uses, the more carbon dioxide it gives off. If the amount of oxygen used by a plant is measured, this would tell us the amount of carbon dioxide given off. The reverse is also true; measuring the amount of carbon dioxide given off tells how much oxygen was used.

When measuring the amount of carbon dioxide given off by a plant, it is helpful to consider these three facts:

1. Carbon dioxide is absorbed, or soaked up, by lime-water and other substances.
2. As carbon dioxide is absorbed by limewater in a closed jar, the pressure inside the jar decreases.
3. As the pressure decreases, the air outside the jar keeps pushing in until the pressure inside the jar is the same as the pressure outside.

In which direction will the oil drop move? Does the direction in which it moves depend upon whether the plant is in darkness or in light? Can this apparatus be used to measure how much carbon dioxide is given off?

## PHOTOSYNTHESIS

Of all the living things on earth, only green plants and a few bacteria are able to make their own food starting from scratch. "Scratch," in this case, means carbon dioxide, water and minerals. The process by which plants make their own food is called *photosynthesis*. "Synthesis" means putting together or manufacturing. Whenever anything is synthesized, or manufactured, energy is needed. The energy needed for food manufacture in green plants comes from light; hence the "photo" part of the name "photosynthesis."

The next few experiments deal with photosynthesis and with some of the factors that affect it. In order to see the effects of these different factors on photosynthesis, it is first necessary to show that photosynthesis is going on.

In this next experiment the rate, or speed, of photosynthesis is measured. One product of photosynthesis is oxygen (read page 21 again). The faster the plant carries on photosynthesis, the faster oxygen is given off.

What happens when a water plant such as *Anacheus* or *Elodea* is placed in water and exposed to light?

What happens if a little bicarbonate of soda is added to the water?

## TURN ON THE LIGHT

Is sunlight the only kind of light that can be used in photosynthesis? Does it matter how far the light is from the plant?

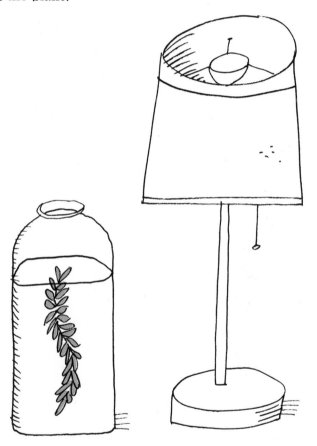

How far from the plant may the lamp be moved and still supply enough light for photosynthesis? Does this distance depend on the brightness of the light?

Different plants need different amounts of light. The common houseplant philodendron does very well with far less light than African violets. If an African violet and a philodendron are placed side by side on the window sill and another African violet and philodendron are placed in a darker corner of the room, what do you notice about their growth? How can the effect of different amounts of light on these plants be judged?

The amount of light plants get varies according to their location and the time of the year. More light falls on plants at the equator than on plants near the North Pole. In the summer, plants receive more light than in the winter. What characteristics of plants can be attributed to the time of year and their geographical location with respect to the amount of light that strikes the plant?

## PICK A COLOR

Does the color of light have an effect on the rate of photosynthesis? How can colored cellophane be used to show such an effect? Try this with several colors.

Which color produces the most rapid rate of photosynthesis? Which color produces the slowest rate?

What is the color of sunlight? Is it the same color all day long? The sunlight of morning and evening is much redder than that of midday. Does this have any influence on the growth of the plant at different times of the day? What will happen to a plant if it is grown under a tent of colored cellophane?

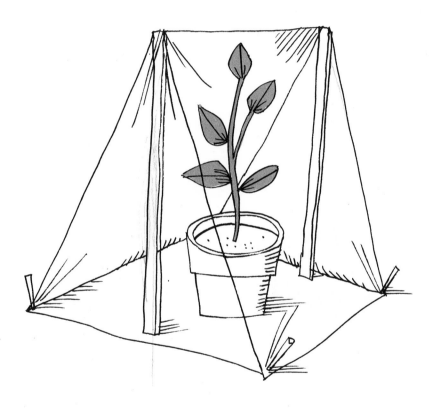

From what you have learned about the effect of color on plants, what would be the best way to grow plants?

## THE HEAT'S ON

How does temperature affect the rate of photosynthesis?

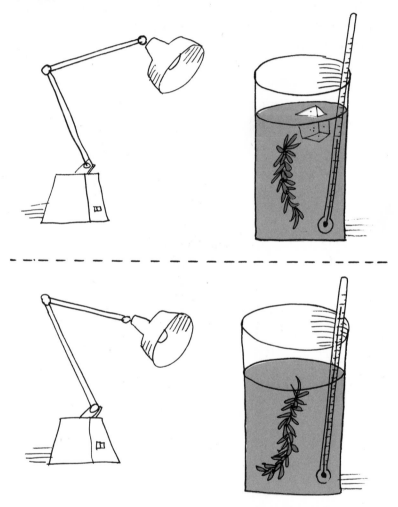

What happens to the plant if it is placed in hot water?

Temperature has a great effect on the rate of photosynthesis. Generally, the warmer the climate in which a plant grows, the more actively the plant carries on photosynthesis and the more the plant grows. This helps explain differences in the length of the growing season in various climates of the world. The growing season in southern California is much longer than it is in North Dakota.

What would happen if a healthy celery plant growing in southern California were transplanted to North Dakota? Why aren't giant redwood trees found in North Dakota? From the type of crop raised in a state, what can one tell about the climate? Cotton is grown in Texas; apples are grown in Vermont. Which crop requires the longer growing season? Could cotton be grown in Vermont? Could apples be grown in Texas?

## PLANT PRODUCTS

Add a few drops of iodine to some starch. What happens? Is there a color change?

This procedure is the chemical test for starch. When iodine is added to any substance, the color change produced shows that starch is present. Is there starch in potatoes? In corn? In apples?

Is there starch in the leaves of plants? Is starch found in leaves that have been covered by aluminum foil for several days?

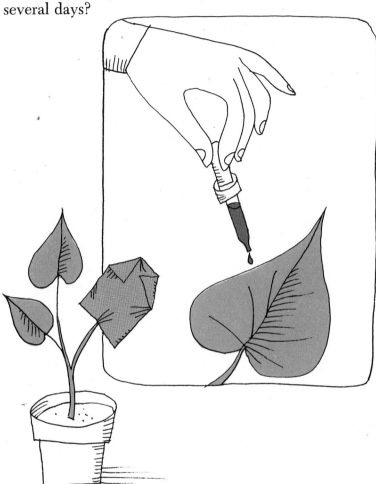

If starch is found in leaves that are exposed to light and not in those that are covered, what might be the relation between photosynthesis and starch production?

## COLOR IT GREEN

Can the green color of a leaf be removed? Grind a leaf with some sand and alcohol. What happens to the color of the alcohol? *Ask an adult to help with this experiment.*

Can you produce the same effect with other liquids?

The substance that gives plants their green color is chlorophyll. Chlorophyll has many unusual characteristics, the most important being that it allows plants to use the energy of light. It does this by reacting in certain ways when light strikes it. By placing the chlorophyll that has been extracted from a leaf in a test tube, you can see one of the characteristics of chlorophyll. Look at the solution in a strong light.

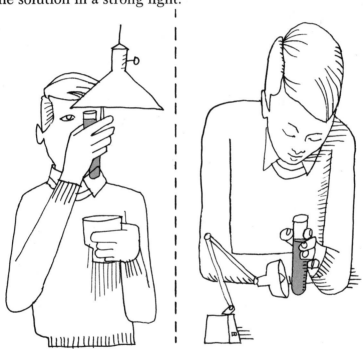

Is there a difference in the color of the solution when you look at it from different directions? What color is seen when you look directly down into the tube? The different colors that are seen are due to the absorption of certain colors of light and not others by the chlorophyll.

## PIGMENT SEPARATION

Chlorophyll is not the only pigment present in plants. The beautiful variety of leaf colors in autumn is due to the loss of chlorophyll. When the chlorophyll disappears from the leaf, other pigments can be seen. These pigments were always present but were hidden by the chlorophyll. The leaf pigments can be seen clearly when they are separated from the chlorophyll. Chemists have found a way to make such a separation. They allow a solution of plant pigments to "climb up" a piece of paper. Different pigments climb at different speeds. Even though they all start climbing at the same. time, they reach different levels at a given time. In this way, they become separated. This method of separation is called chromatography.

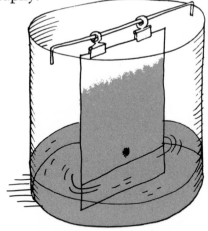

What liquid is best to use in the bottom of the jar? Does alcohol work as well as carbon tetrachloride (cleaning fluid)?

*Ask an adult to help you with this one!*

Try separating pigments extracted from a leaf. Evaporating the pigment solution will make the pigments more concentrated and they will work best in this form. Put a small drop of concentrated pigment solution on a piece of white blotting paper and allow it to dry. Do this spotting at the same place on the paper about ten times and allow it to dry between spottings. Keep the drops very small.

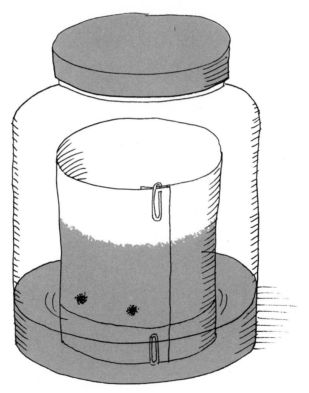

What happens if a drop of tomato juice or carrot juice is used in place of the pigment solution?

## PIGMENT PRODUCTION

Do covered leaves have the same pigments as leaves that are uncovered? Try extracting and separating the pigments of a leaf that has been covered with aluminum foil. Does the length of time the leaf has been covered have any influence on the kind or amount of pigments found?

Does the kind of plant that is used have any effect on the results? Try using *Coleus* or some other plant with multicolored leaves.

The pigments in leaves are needed for the production of starch. But just because the leaves have pigments does not mean that starch will be made. There are other requirements. In addition to the pigments, the plant needs a combination of light, water and nutrients to carry on photosynthesis and produce starch.

Can photosynthesis be carried on if chlorophyll, carbon dioxide and water in a test tube are exposed to light? In what way can you tell if photosynthesis is working in such a test tube? Don't be disappointed if you can't get it to work. No one else can, either!

## PIGMENT DISTRIBUTION

Do the various parts of plants produce pigments? Are there pigments in stems? Are they the same as those in the leaf? It is possible to find out whether pigments are present by scraping material from the surface of different parts of the plant and extracting them with alcohol.

Are there pigments in roots?

Leaves are not the only part of the plant in which photosynthesis takes place. The process of photosynthesis is found anywhere in plants where chlorophyll is found. There are many plants in which a great deal of photosynthesis takes place in the stems. Examples of such plants are celery, corn and rhubarb. In these, the stem is as important as, or more important than, the leaf in the production of food.

While the stem and the leaf carry out photosynthesis in most plants, the root does not. You have seen that roots do not contain chlorophyll or other pigments and so it is easy to understand why photosynthesis does not occur in roots. Yet many roots contain large amounts of food produced by photosynthesis. Two questions arise:

1. How do roots obtain food if the food is manufactured in some other part of the plant?
2. Why is there no chlorophyll in the root?

The answer to the second question may be found by looking at the experiment in "Pigment Production."

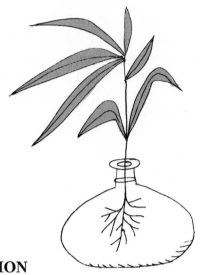

## STARCH DIGESTION

The chemical reactions taking place in plants, and in animals too, are regulated and controlled by chemicals known as enzymes. In the next few pages, you will find experiments that deal with these important chemicals.

Enzymes work by speeding up chemical reactions. An example of this is the action of enzymes in sprouting corn seeds. Here the enzymes are able to help change starches to sugars. To demonstrate this change, you must be able to know when starches have been changed to something else. By adding a few drops of iodine to a little flour in water, you will be able to see a color change. Add some takadiastase, an enzyme preparation that can be purchased in any drugstore, to a fresh solution of starch and water. Allow it to stand for a while and then test the solution with iodine. What happens? Does it matter how much starch is used? Does it matter how much enzyme is used? Does it matter how long the enzyme acts on the starch? Does it matter if the solution is warm or cold when the enzyme is added?

Does a sprouting corn seed contain any enzymes that will change starch to some other compound? Find out by grinding several sprouting corn seeds and adding them to a weak solution of starch and water. After allowing the mixture to stand for some time, it can be tested with iodine for the presence of starch.

Do corn seeds contain starch? If so, what is the job of the enzyme during sprouting?

## ENZYMES

Are enzymes found in all plant materials? What happens if a small piece of potato is placed in a glass containing hydrogen peroxide?

Will this reaction work if a piece of plant stem is used? Will this reaction work if a piece of root is used?

When a certain enzyme found in potatoes is added to hydrogen peroxide, the reaction that follows results in breaking down the hydrogen peroxide and releasing bubbles of oxygen. Find out if the bubbles are oxygen by thrusting a glowing splint or matchstick into the glass. If the splint bursts into flame, this is considered to be a positive test for oxygen. *Ask an adult to help you with this.*

The enzyme responsible for the reaction shown above is called catalase. It is found in a wide variety of plants and is important in removing hydrogen peroxide, a by-product of photosynthesis in plants. If the hydrogen peroxide were to collect in large amounts, it would injure the plant. Therefore, in this case, the enzyme catalase does an important job in preventing the buildup of a harmful substance in the plant.

Do apples contain catalase? Do carrots? Radishes? Bananas? Lettuce?

## ENZYME REACTION RATE

What happens if a piece of cooked potato is added to some hydrogen peroxide?

What happens if a piece of ice-cold raw potato is added to cold hydrogen peroxide?

One of the most important factors controlling enzyme activity is temperature. From the three experiments just completed, it can be seen that if the temperature is too low or too high the enzyme does not work well. In between "too high" and "too low" is some temperature at which the enzyme functions best. This temperature is called the optimum temperature. To find out what the optimum temperature is, it must first be decided what is meant by "functions best." Usually it means how fast the reaction takes place.

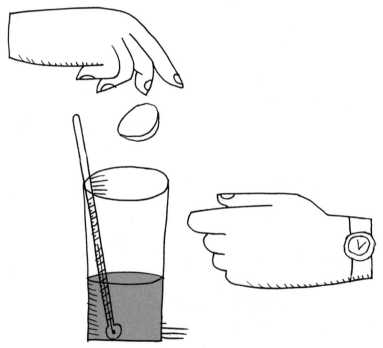

Find the optimum temperature for the action of potato catalase. How can the speed of the reaction be found?

## ENZYMES AND SALTS

What happens when a piece of raw potato that has been soaked in strong salt water for several hours is added to a glass of hydrogen peroxide?

What happens when a piece of raw potato that has been soaked in liquid bleach is placed in some hydrogen peroxide?

Enzymes are sensitive to many different chemicals in the way that you have just observed. When enzymes come into contact with certain other compounds, the enzymes are in some way changed. The chemical which changes the enzyme and stops its action is called an inhibitor.

Many common chemicals act as enzyme inhibitors. Try to find some enzyme inhibitors that are available in your home. Start with such items as disinfectants, soaps, detergents and other household cleaners. *Have an adult help you select the chemicals you use.*

While experimenting, be certain to consider the amount of each substance used. For example, it might be found that a small amount of a substance has no effect while a large amount would slow down enzyme action.

Soak a piece of raw potato in some water in which some copper pennies have been placed. What happens when this piece of potato is placed in some hydrogen peroxide?

## ENZYMES, ACIDS AND BASES

Do strong acids have any effect on the actions of catalase?

Do strong bases have any effect on the actions of catalase?

Acids and bases have a definite effect on enzymes. Remember that extremes of temperature inhibit the action of enzymes. Extremes of acids and bases have the same effect. Between the extremes of "very acid" and "very basic" there is an optimum point at which enzymes work best. The optimum point is different for each different enzyme. Can you find the optimum acid or base level for catalase? Vinegar added to water in varying amounts will provide a range of solutions with different degrees of acidity.

A range of base solutions can be made by adding varying amounts of bicarbonate of soda to water.

## AUXINS

Have you ever noticed how plants turn toward the light?

What happens if young plants are placed in boxes like those shown here?

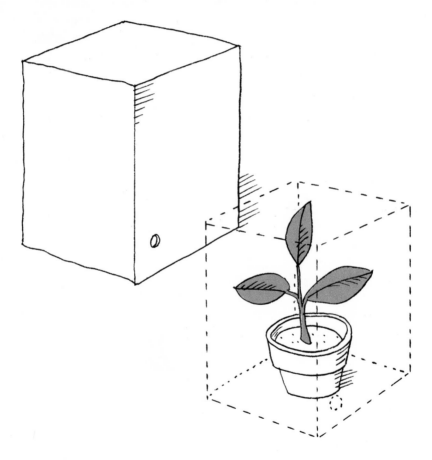

What happens if the plant is placed in a box with no hole in it?

The turning and bending movements of plants are brought about by substances produced within the plant. These substances are called auxins. Auxins are sometimes called plant hormones because they act in plants in the same way hormones act in animals; that is, they control or regulate the growth of the plant.

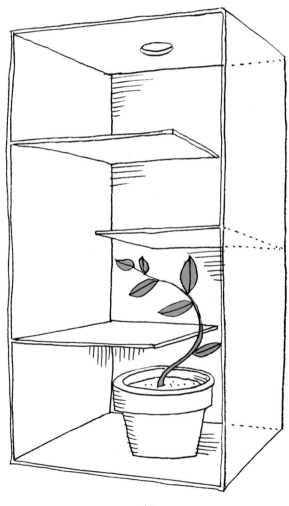

## AUXINS AGAIN

What happens when auxins mixed with lanolin are smeared on one side of a plant stem? Auxins are sold as rooting aids at garden supply stores.

What happens if the tip of the plant is cut off before the auxin-lanolin mixture is smeared on?

Does it make a difference if the side of the stem is gently scraped before the auxin-lanolin mixture is applied?

After auxins were discovered, it was thought that they might act only on one part of the plant and only in one way. This was very soon shown to be wrong. There are many auxins that are known to botanists. Each one is somewhat different from the others and causes different responses in plants. In fact, a specific auxin may even cause different responses in different parts of a plant. For example, it might cause the root to do one thing and the stem to do the opposite.

Auxins are used by gardeners to speed up root formation in cuttings and transplants and are also used as weed-killers. What accounts for the fact that auxins can bring about such opposite effects as growth and death? Part of the answer is that the effect of auxins depends on the concentration or amount used. In very low concentrations, the auxins cause growth, bending and turning movements and other helpful actions. But in high concentrations, they upset the metabolism of plants and cause them to grow too rapidly and too unevenly; in a sense, the plants grow themselves to death.

Why is it then, that weed-killers kill weeds but not the lawn grass that the gardener wants to keep?

## MIGHTY LIKE AN AUXIN

What happens to a plant when it is treated with gibberellic acid? Gibberellic acid may be purchased at garden supply stores. It can be used on plants by making a solution of the substance in water and applying the solution to the leaves.

What happens when the solution is applied to the top of the plant? To the tip of a branch? Midway down the stem?

Gibberellic acid is one of the group of substances whose general name is gibberellins. They are produced by certain fungi and have also been synthesized in laboratories. The gibberellins have a drastic effect on the growth of plants, causing a great increase in size.

Gibberellic acid is of great economic importance because, used together with auxins, it can be used to help plants produce larger fruits and flowers than normal. Another important use of these substances is to cause seeds to germinate earlier than they normally would.

What happens if gibberellic acid is applied to dwarf varieties of plants?

Is it possible that Jack's beanstalk was the result of gibberellic acid treatment?

## MATERIAL SOURCES

*Garden Supply Stores or Nurseries*
Seeds, auxins, gibberellic acid, pots, plants (Philodendron, African Violets, *Coleus*)

*Hardware Stores and Supermarkets*
Thermometer, paper cups, food coloring, paraffin, detergent, salad oil, plastic bags, straws (the narrower the better), sodium bicarbonate, colored cellophane (red, yellow, green, blue), glass tumblers, aluminum foil, blotting paper, tomato juice, cleaning fluid, vinegar, liquid bleach.

*Drugstores*
Petroleum jelly, limewater, iodine, alcohol, takadiastase, hydrogen peroxide, test tubes

*Aquarium Supply Stores*
*Anacheus, Elodea*

# GLOSSARY

ACID—Substance that reacts with a base to form a salt. Acids usually have a sour or bitter taste. Many household liquids are acids; for example, lemon juice, vinegar and soda pop. The sharp or tart taste of many foods (rhubarb, strawberry, orange) is due to acids they contain.

AUXIN—A special type of plant hormone. Auxins cause elongation of plant cells. This results in bending movements of the stem and roots, and also produces lengthening of the stem. Auxins are produced in plants and are effective in very low concentrations. They are used by gardeners as rooting aids and to make plants grow more quickly. In higher concentrations, auxins cause an upset in plant metabolism, resulting in the plant's death. Many weed killers are auxins used in high concentrations.

BASE—Chemical that reacts with an acid to form a salt.

Some bases have a salty taste, some a bitter taste, and some have no special taste. Common household substances that are bases are ammonia, baking soda and oven cleaner. *Caution: Do not test the taste of ammonia or oven cleaner.*

CATALASE—An enzyme that brings about the chemical breakdown of hydrogen peroxide. The reaction results in the formation of water and oxygen. Catalase is found in many different plants, animals and bacteria. Its name indicates that catalase is an enzyme since most enzymes have names ending in "ase." Some examples of enzymes are maltase, which digests malt sugar; lipase, which digests fats; amylase, which digests starch; and takadiastase, the starch-digesting enzyme used in "Starch Digestion."

CHLOROPHYLL—The green pigment found in plants. It is essential for the process of photosynthesis. Chlorophyll acts by harnessing the energy of light and allowing plants to use that energy for chemical reactions. These reactions are photosynthesis. See PHOTOSYNTHESIS.

CHROMATOGRAPHY—A procedure used to separate various substances in a mixture. There are many different techniques that may be used, one of the most common being paper chromatography. In this procedure, a mixture of substances is treated in such a way that all of the substances move through paper that has been moistened by a solvent. Each different substance moves through the paper at its own rate. In a given interval of time, the fastest substance will have moved farthest from the original point, while the slowest one will have moved only a short distance. In between these, the other substances will be strung out. The substances therefore become separated according to the speed with which they travel through the moistened paper.

CONCENTRATION—Refers to the amount of solid material that has been dissolved in a liquid. A glass of water with one spoonful of sugar dissolved in it is *less concentrated* than a glass of water with two spoonfuls of sugar dissolved in it.

CONTROL—A test similar to the experiment in all ways except for the one factor being tested. Experiments are designed to test a single condition or factor. This single condition or factor is the only thing that is changed during the experiment; everything else remains constant. In the control, this factor is omitted. Therefore the control shows what would have happened if the factor being tested had not been changed. A control allows the researcher to tell whether or not his results really are due to the test factor.

DIGESTION—The process during which foods are broken down into simpler compounds by the action of enzymes. These simpler compounds are soluble in the liquid portion of the plant; namely, water. In this soluble form, these food substances are carried throughout the plant and are used by it. Digestion occurs in similar fashion in animals.

ENZYME—Proteins that control the rate of chemical reactions. Chemical reactions in plants are greatly speeded up by enzymes. Each enzyme is able to catalyze or speed up only one particular reaction and is said to be *specific* for that reaction. Enzymes are not used up in the reactions they control, so a little bit of enzyme goes a long way.

GERMINATION—The initial growth of a seed. Seeds start to germinate, or sprout, only under favorable conditions. These conditions vary for different kinds of seeds. One kind of seed may need a good deal of moisture in order to germinate; another kind may need a spell of cold weather before sprouting. Temperature, light factors and other conditions are also important in the germination of seeds.

HORMONE—A chemical that is produced in one part of a plant or animal body and carried to another part of the body, where it controls or regulates activity. Hormones are effective in extremely low concentrations. The kinds of effects produced by hormones are quite varied; some cause increased growth of stem or root, some control leaf-fall and some control the dropping of fruit.

HUMIDITY—The water vapor or moisture contained in the air. It is usually measured as a percentage of the total amount of water that could be contained when the air is at a given temperature. The humidity is 50% when the air at any temperature holds half as much moisture as it could possibly contain. Plants contribute a large quantity of moisture to the air.

INHIBITOR—Any chemical substance which acts to slow down, block, or stop a reaction from occurring. There are other ways of blocking reactions in plants. Excessive heat or cold may also slow down reactions.

METABOLISM—All the chemical reactions taking place in plants. Plants use food materials to make more of themselves; that is, to repair damage and to grow. These activities and all others, including flowering and fruit formation, are brought about by chemical reactions.

OPTIMUM—The best or most favorable condition for plant growth is called the optimum condition. Many factors must be considered in obtaining the optimum condition for plant growth. The optimum condition is the best balance of light intensity, temperature, moisture, nutrients and other factors.

PHOTOSYNTHESIS—The process by which green plants combine carbon dioxide and water to make food. Chlorophyll is required for the process, and oxygen is given off as a by-product. In addition to chlorophyll, light and certain enzymes are essential. Photosynthesis results in the formation of simple sugars, which are then converted to complex sugars, starch, proteins and other substances that are stored and used by the plant.

PIGMENT—Any substance which gives color to other substances.

SOLVENT—A liquid in which some substance is dissolved. Water, for example, is a solvent for sugar, table salt and a large number of materials. Because it is so common in the natural world and dissolves so many materials, water is one of the most important solvents known. Water is the most abundant material in plants and acts as a solvent for many important plant substances.

STOMATE—A tiny opening in the surface of leaves and stems. Through the stomates, gases such as oxygen, carbon dioxide and water vapor pass. The size of the opening is regulated by a pair of cells, called guard cells, that surround the stomate. The amount of gas that may enter or leave the plant depends upon the size of the stomate. Under dry conditions, the stomates are small, allowing very little water vapor to leave. In this way, water is conserved by the plant.

SYNTHESIS—Any process in which two or more substances are combined to form a new and larger substance.

TURGIDITY—Describes that characteristic of a plant which can be called "stiffness." The turgidity of a plant depends upon the amount of water the plant contains. If it has sufficient water, the plant will be turgid; if not, it will be limp and wilted.